THE ADVENTURES OF MOLLY

School Therapy Dog Extraordinaire

WRITTEN AND ILLUSTRATED BY
KAILEE POTTER

DrKP Books

THE ADVENTURES OF MOLLY

For Preston, Maevryn, and Augustus.
I love you all dearly.
Additionally, thank you Molly, for all the joy you bring.

Hi! My name is Molly. My life is amazing. Every day I get to go on new adventures with my mom. She says I am a School Therapy Dog! When we go to school, everyone knows my name and loves to stop and pet me. But I am getting ahead of myself, let's start from the beginning!

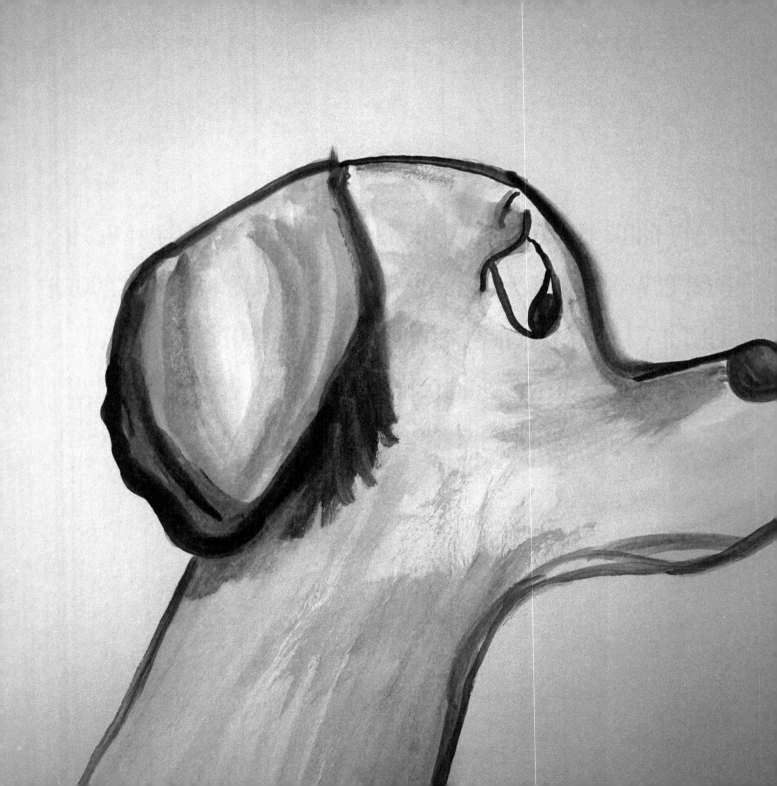

I don't know much about when I was young. I was found roaming the streets and taken to a shelter. That was scary, but I was so happy to be found and safe at last.

One day a nice lady named Bella came and interviewed me at the shelter. That means she asked a lot of questions and spent a lot of time getting to know me. I guess, she figured out how amazing I am. Next thing I knew I was headed to her farm!

OPERATION SCHOOLHOUSE

The farm I went to is called Operation Schoolhouse. Bella explained that I was going to have an important job one day and we needed to work hard training.

I spent months learning my new job. I learned how to sit, stay, visit, comfort, leave it, and find my bed. I worked really hard and never gave up!

One day I overheard Bella talking. She said there was a match for me. What could that mean?

A few days later, two women came to the farm. They waited in the cabin as Bella came for me.

When I walked into the cabin, I knew I had found my mom! She was waiting with open arms and cried a little too!

We immediately began the process of working as a team. I knew my mom was just right for me. Her name is Dr. Kailee Potter.

A few weeks later we walked into school on a Saturday for the first time together as Mom and Therapy Dog team. I was so excited!

To get ready for my debut, my mom created a slideshow for students and gave everyone a lot of information about me.

On my first day of school, I met with many different kids and adults. All of them were great and loved me! And I loved them!

Since starting with my mom, I have visited hundreds of children. Sometimes they are happy, sad, upset, or frustrated. I always help them to be calm.

I take my job very seriously. I will not play when I am working. Instead, I listen to mom's commands and follow her directions.

Sometimes, I get to take my special vest off at work. Then I know it is okay to play. But once my vest is back on, I am back in work mode.

I have a safe space in mom's office, my bed. I stay on it to let others know I am working or resting.

Sometimes I like to sleep on my mom's bean bag. She doesn't seem to mind.

Every day is a bit different, but I like it that way. I love my job and all the humans I get to see!

I have made so many great memories already, I cannot wait to see what adventures in helping come next!

Printed in the USA
CPSIA information can be obtained
at www.ICGtesting.com
CBHW081026240724
12037CB00023B/703

9 798218 465971